Presented to

_____

by

_____

on

_____

To Jacqueline Marie Bowman:

Thank you for making me a grandma!

My Grandma & Me

TYNDALE KiDS

Tyndale House Publishers, Inc.
Carol Stream, Illinois

written by Crystal Bowman
Illustrated by Katherine Kirkland

Visit Tyndale's website for kids at www.tyndale.com/kids.

Visit Crystal Bowman's website at www.crystalbowman.com.

TYNDALE KIDS and the Tyndale Kids logo are registered trademarks of Tyndale House Publishers, Inc.

My Grandma and Me: Rhyming Devotions for You and Your Grandchild

Designed by Jacqueline L. Nuñez

Edited by Betty Free Swanberg

Unless otherwise indicated, all Scripture quotations are taken from the *Holy Bible*, New Living Translation, copyright © 1996, 2004, 2007 by Tyndale House Foundation. Used by permission of Tyndale House Publishers, Inc., Carol Stream, Illinois 60188. All rights reserved.

Scripture quotations marked NKJV are taken from the New King James Version.® Copyright © 1982 by Thomas Nelson, Inc. Used by permission. All rights reserved. *NKJV* is a trademark of Thomas Nelson, Inc.

Scripture quotations marked "ICB" are taken from the International Children's Bible.® Copyright © 1986, 1988, 1999 by Thomas Nelson, Inc. Used by permission. All rights reserved. *ICB* is a trademark of Thomas Nelson, Inc.

Scripture quotations marked NIrV are taken from the Holy Bible, *New International Reader's Version,*® NIrV.® Copyright © 1995, 1996, 1998 by Biblica, Inc.™ Used by permission of Zondervan. All rights reserved worldwide. www.zondervan.com.

Scripture quotations marked NIV are taken from the Holy Bible, *New International Version,*® NIV.® Copyright © 1973, 1978, 1984, 2011 by Biblica, Inc.™ Used by permission of Zondervan. All rights reserved worldwide. www.zondervan.com.

For manufacturing information regarding this product, please call 1-800-323-9400.

Library of Congress Cataloging-in-Publication Data

Bowman, Crystal.

  My grandma and me : rhyming devotions for you and your grandchild / Crystal Bowman.

    p. cm.

  ISBN 978-1-4143-7170-2

1. Children—Prayers and devotions—Juvenile literature. 2. Grandparent and child—Religious aspects—Christianity. 3. Grandmothers. I. Title

  BV4870.B69 2012

  249—dc23

2012011646

Printed in China

18	17	16	15	14	13	12
7	6	5	4	3	2	1

Contents

How to Use This Book

"Did God really make me special, Grandma?"

Yes, he did! You are special because there is no one else like you in the whole world. You are special because God loves you very much!"

Wouldn't you love to have a conversation like that with your grandchild? You can! And this book can prompt many other precious talks with the little ones in your life.

As grandmothers, we can have a positive influence on the spiritual development of our grandchildren. Have you ever heard of Grandmother Lois? In 2 Timothy 1:5, the apostle Paul writes to Timothy, his young understudy, who was the pastor to the church in Ephesus, "I remember your genuine faith, for you share the faith that first filled your grandmother Lois and your mother, Eunice. And I know that same faith continues strong in you."

So according to this verse, Grandmother Lois became a follower of Christ, and she shared her faith with her daughter Eunice and her grandson Timothy. And God felt this was worth mentioning in the Holy Scriptures? Yes.

As we raise our children in the Lord, we teach them and train them and pray that they will share our faith and stay strong as they become adults. But our job is not finished when our children grow up. When grandchildren arrive, we have another opportunity to teach and train little ones in the Lord, just as Grandmother Lois did.

The purpose of this book is to offer Bible verses, mini-lessons, prayers, songs, and familiar Bible passages for grandmothers to share with their grandchildren. As you hold your little ones in your lap, you can help them understand more about who God is and how much he loves them. The interactive text allows you and your grandchildren to recite and memorize short Bible verses, pray prayers together, and sing songs. You may choose to read one selection at a time or read several pages if you have an attentive listener.

But what if Grandma's lap is too far away? In today's culture, many grandmothers are separated geographically from their grandchildren. The answer is found in modern technology, which allows loved ones to stay close. Grandmothers can use this book to connect with their grandchildren over the telephone or by video chatting online. A grandmother in the United States can share this book with her granddaughter in Russia. A grandmother in Maine can share this book with her grandson in California. Since many grandparents are already connecting with their grandchildren in this way, this book can help to make that time more precious.

Telephone Time: Choose a specific time to talk each week. If you and your grandchild each have a copy of the book, you can look at the same page at the same time. You can read several of the selections as time allows. Agree to memorize the Bible verse or verses that you read together, and confirm the next phone date before saying good-bye. Then begin the next telephone time by reciting the verse or verses you memorized.

Online Video Chat (Skype): The added benefit of an online video chat is that it allows face-to-face communication with your grandchild. You can read the book to your grandchild while showing him or her the pictures on the screen. If your grandchild has a book as well, you can take turns selecting the pages to be read. Choose a specific time to video chat each week, and make your time together fun and meaningful.

There are many creative and useful ways to use this book. But the best reason for using this book is to pass down your faith to future generations, as we read in Psalm 78:4: "We will not hide these truths from our children; we will tell the next generation about the glorious deeds of the LORD, about his power and his mighty wonders."

May God bless you as you teach the little ones in your life to follow him.

—Crystal Bowman

Rhyming Devotions

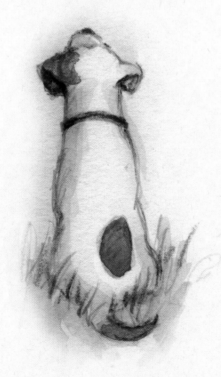

God Made It All

The Bible Says:

In the beginning God created the heavens and the earth.

Genesis 1:1

God is great! He said the words
that made the flowers and the birds.
He made the moon to shine at night.
He made the sun to give us light.

He made the stars up in the sky.
He made the mountains, big and high.
He made the land. He made the sea.
He made it all for you and me.

Sing with Me:

Tune: "Twinkle, Twinkle, Little Star"

Lord, you made the birds that fly,
and you made the big, blue sky.
Rivers, flowers, grass, and trees,
butterflies and honeybees.
Thank you, God, for all I see.
Thank you, God, for making me.

God Cares about You

The Bible Says:

If God cares so wonderfully for wildflowers . . .
he will certainly care for you.

Matthew 6:30

God cares about each living thing,
like flowers growing in the spring.
He gives them rain and sunshine, too,
so surely God will care for you.

God helps the birds to build a nest
so they can have a place to rest.
He gives them food and water, too,
so surely God will care for you.

Pray with Me:

Dear God, thank you for sending rain to help the grass and flowers grow. Thank you for helping the birds find food to eat. Thank you for taking care of me and helping me to grow too. Please bless my grandma and my whole family. In Jesus' name, amen.

No More Worries

The Bible Says:

Don't worry about anything. Instead, tell God about everything.

Philippians 4:6, NIrV

Do you wonder what you'll be
when you're twelve or twenty-three?
God will help you figure out
what your life will be about.

Tell God what is on your mind.
He will help you. He is kind.
If you're big or if you're small,
do not worry—not at all.

Pray with Me:

Dear God, thank you that I never have to worry about anything.
All I need to do is ask, and you will always help me.
In Jesus' name, amen.

God Is with You

The Bible Says:

I know the LORD is always with me.
I will not be shaken, for he is right beside me.

Psalm 16:8

You can run, and you can hide.
You can jump, and you can slide.
And no matter what you do,
God is always there with you!

You can travel on a plane,
in a car, or on a train.
On the ground or in the air—
God is with you everywhere.

Sing with Me:

Tune: "Mary Had a Little Lamb"

God is with me every day,
every day, every day.
When I sleep or work or play,
he's with me every day.

God is with me every day,
every day, every day.
If I'm home or far away,
he's with me every day.

Pray to God

The Bible Says:

God, I call out to you because you will answer me.
Listen to me. Hear my prayer.

Psalm 17:6, NIrV

God will always hear your prayer.
He will listen. He will care.
On your knees or standing tall,
tell him anything at all.

Just remember when you pray,
God will answer his own way.
God knows what is best for you.
Wait to see what he will do.

Pray with Me:

Dear God, thank you that I can pray to you and tell you anything.
I know that you care about me very much and that you will
always do what is best. Thank you for listening to me when I pray.
In Jesus' name, amen.

A Very Special Book

The Bible Says:

Open my eyes to see the wonderful things in your teachings.

Psalm 119:18, ICB

The Bible is a special book,
with lots of stories—take a look!
It tells us how the world began.
God made a woman and a man.

The Bible tells us how to live—
how to share and help and give.
The Bible says that God loves you,
and God wants you to love him, too.

Pray with Me:

Thank you, God, for my Bible. Your words tell me all about you
and how much you love me. Help me to learn more about you
from your special book. In Jesus' name, amen.

You Are Special

The Bible Says:

I praise you because you made me in an amazing and wonderful way.

Psalm 139:14, ICB

God made your eyes. He made your nose,
your fingers, and your little toes.
God made your hair. He made your face.
He put your ears in the right place.

He made your mouth. He made your chin.
He made your elbows and your skin.
He made you on the inside, too.
God made you special, through and through.

Sing with Me:

Tune: "The B-I-B-L-E"

God made just one of me.
I'm special, can't you see?
He made my eyes and ears and nose.
He made each part of me.

Say You're Sorry

The Bible Says:

I am deeply sorry for what I have done.

Psalm 38:18

Did you know it makes God sad
whenever you do something bad?
So if you ever disobey,
say you're sorry right away.

Try to do what's right and good.
Try to please God, as you should.
God will help you to obey.
Ask him now—he'll help today.

Pray with Me:

Dear God, thank you for loving me even when I do things that I
should not do. I am sorry for the things I do that are wrong.
Please forgive me, and help me to do what is right and kind and good.
In Jesus' name, amen.

Don't Be Afraid

The Bible Says:

God has come to save me. I will trust in him and not be afraid.

Isaiah 12:2

When the rain comes falling down
and the wind blows all around,
do not fear the noisy storm.
God can keep you safe and warm.

Do not be afraid at night.
God will send the morning light.
Talk to God. He's always near.
You can whisper—he will hear.

Pray with Me:

Dear God, when I am afraid, I will talk to you. I know you are always with me and you will help me to be brave. Thank you for watching over me all the time. In Jesus' name, amen.

Be Happy

The Bible Says:

A glad heart makes a happy face.

Proverbs 15:13

You can have a happy heart.
Loving God is where you start.
There's no reason to stay sad.
Sing to God—he'll make you glad.

Clap your hands and sing a song.
Lift your feet and march along.
Turn your frown into a smile.
Make it last a long, long while.

Sing with Me:

Tune: "Twinkle, Twinkle, Little Star"

I will sing a happy song;
I'll be happy all day long.
With a smile upon my face,
I'll be happy any place.
If I'm ever feeling sad,
I will sing and soon be glad.

Be a Helper

The Bible Says:

Work willingly at whatever you do, as though you were working for the Lord rather than for people.

Colossians 3:23

When you help to do the chores,
like folding clothes or sweeping floors,
do the best that you can do.
Then God will be so pleased with you.

Put your toys where they belong.
Make your bed—it won't take long.
After all your chores are done,
you can play and have some fun!

Pray with Me:

Dear Lord Jesus, please help me to be a good helper. I know you are pleased when I do my best for you. Help me to do my chores with a smile on my face. Amen.

God Wants You to Share

The Bible Says:

If you have extra clothes, you should share with those who have none.
And if you have extra food, you should do the same.

Luke 3:11, NIrV

Sometimes there are girls and boys
who don't have many clothes or toys.
Share your crayons. Share your blocks.
You can share your shoes and socks.

Sometimes kids need food to eat.
Share a sandwich or a treat.
God is happy when you share,
so share with people everywhere.

Pray with Me:

Dear God, thank you for my food, my clothes, and my toys. Please help the people who don't have what they need. Help me to share with boys and girls who don't have as much as I do. In Jesus' name, amen.

Love One Another

The Bible Says:

Dear friends, let us love one another, because love comes from God.

1 John 4:7, NIrV

It is good to love each other;
love your sister and your brother.
Love your neighbors down the street.
Love the new friends that you meet.

God's the one who gives us love.
It's a blessing from above.
Thank him for the love he sends.
His love is great—it never ends.

Sing with Me:

Tune: "Twinkle, Twinkle, Little Star"

Thank you, Father, for your love
that you send from up above.
Fill my heart with love for you.
Help me to love others, too.
I'll be very kind today
as I help and as I play.

Say Thank You to God

The Bible Says:

Give thanks to the Lord for his faithful love.

Psalm 107:8, NIrV

The clothes you have, the food you eat,
the shoes you wear on both your feet,
the sunny days with sky so blue
are blessings that God gives to you.

So thank him, every time you pray,
for all he gives you every day.
Tell God what you're thankful for.
He will bless you more and more.

Pray with Me:

Dear God, thank you for food to eat and clothes to wear.
Thank you for my family and friends. Thank you for the sun and rain
and for birds that sing and stars that shine. But most of all,
thank you for your love for me. In Jesus' name, amen.

Have a Good Day

The Bible Says:

This is the day the LORD has made. We will rejoice and be glad in it.

Psalm 118:24

God makes every single day!
You can sing and dance and play.
You can climb, and you can run.
You can laugh and have some fun.

In the morning, when you rise,
open up your sleepy eyes.
Thank the Lord for all you see,
and say, "God made this day for me!"

Sing with Me:

Tune: "Mary Had a Little Lamb"

Thank you for this special day,
special day, special day.
Thank you for this special day.
You made it just for me.

Lord, I love this happy day,
happy day, happy day.
Lord, I love this happy day.
I'm happy as can be!

Care about Others

The Bible Says:

Take tender care of those who are weak.

1 Thessalonians 5:14

When your friends are sick or sad,
cheer them up, and make them glad.
Draw a picture. Make a card.
Pick a flower from the yard.

Tell your friends you'll say a prayer.
That will let them know you care.
Jesus cares so much for you.
You should care for others, too.

Pray with Me:

Dear Jesus, thank you that you care about everyone.
Help me to care about others the way you care for me. Help my friends
who are sick, and help those who are sad. Please help me show others
that I care about them. In your name, amen.

God Keeps His Promises

The Bible Says:

The LORD always keeps his promises.

Psalm 145:13

God promises to be with you,
to care for you and help you too.
God promises that when you pray,
he'll listen to each word you say.

God promises to be your friend.
His love for you will never end.
He'll keep his promises to you.
That's what the Bible says he'll do.

Sing with Me:

Tune: "Mary Had a Little Lamb"

Thank you for your promises,
promises, promises—
all the special promises
you give to me each day.

Lord, I love your promises,
promises, promises.
Lord, I love your promises.
Thank you, Lord, I pray.

God Is So Great!

The Bible Says:

You are great. You do wonderful things. You alone are God.

Psalm 86:10, NIrV

Look into the great big sky.
See the heavens way up high?
See the clouds and see the sun?
God put them there for everyone.

The sun comes up to start the day,
and then at night, it hides away.
God is great, and that is why
only God could make the sky!

Pray with Me:

Dear God, thank you that I can look into the sky and see
how great you are. You made the sun so we can have light during
the daytime. You made the nighttime so we can sleep. You are great
and wonderful. In Jesus' name, amen.

Give Praise to God

The Bible Says:

God is the King over all the earth. Praise him with a psalm.

Psalm 47:7

God is Lord, and he is King;
that is why we praise and sing.
Lift your hands up to the sky.
Praise the Lord, our King on high.

Use your voice to sing out loud—
by yourself or in a crowd.
Sing to God and give him praise.
Thank him for his awesome ways.

Sing with Me:

Tune: "Twinkle, Twinkle, Little Star"

Lord, you are my God and King.
You are King of everything.
I will praise you with my song.
I will thank you all day long.
I will lift my hands and sing.
I will praise my Lord and King.

God Loves the World

The Bible Says:

God loved the world so much that he gave his one and only Son.
Anyone who believes in him will not die but will have eternal life.

John 3:16, NIrV

God sent Jesus, his own Son,
because God loves us, every one.
Jesus came from heaven to earth.
The angels told about his birth.

He died to save the world from sin,
but Jesus came to life again.
Believe in Jesus, God's own Son,
who died to save us, every one.

Pray with Me:

Dear God, thank you for sending Jesus to die for my sins.
I'm sorry about the bad things that I have done. I want Jesus
to help me do what is right. In Jesus' name, amen.

Jesus Loves You

The Bible Says:

Let the children come to me. Don't stop them! For the Kingdom of God belongs to those who are like these children.

Mark 10:14

The children sat on Jesus' knee.
He said, "Please let them come to me."
He wanted everyone to know
he cared for them and loved them so.

Jesus still loves kids today.
He loves to hear them sing and pray.
So tell your friends he loves them, too.
That is something you can do.

Sing with Me:

Song: "Jesus Loves Me!"

Jesus loves me! This I know,
for the Bible tells me so.
Little ones to him belong.
They are weak but he is strong.

Yes, Jesus loves me!
Yes, Jesus loves me!
Yes, Jesus loves me!
The Bible tells me so.

You Are God's Child

The Bible Says:

See how very much our Father loves us, for he calls us his children,
and that is what we are!

1 John 3:1

If you love Jesus, you can be
a part of God's own family.
Grandmas, grandpas, dads, and mothers,
aunts and uncles, sisters, brothers.

Young and old and big and small,
in heaven there is room for all.
Aren't you happy you can be
a child in God's family?

Pray with Me:

Dear God, thank you for being my special Father in heaven.
I know you love me very much. Thank you that I am your child and
that I can be with you in heaven someday. In Jesus' name, amen.

Tell Others about Jesus

The Bible Says:

Tell about all the wonderful things [the Lord] has done.

Psalm 105:2, ICB

Everybody needs to know
what Jesus did so long ago.
He healed the sick and calmed the sea.
He helped the blind so they could see.

He healed the lame so they could walk.
He helped the ones who couldn't talk.
So tell your friends that he is great.
Tell them soon, and do not wait!

Sing with Me:

Tune: "Mary Had a Little Lamb"

Jesus is so wonderful,
wonderful, wonderful.
I will tell how good he is
to all my friends today.

Everybody needs to know,
needs to know, needs to know.
Everybody needs to know
of Jesus' love today.

Be like Jesus

The Bible Says:

Live a life filled with love, following the example of Christ.

Ephesians 5:2

Jesus loves you. This is true!
Be like him in all you do.
Be polite. Be kind and good.
Treat your friends the way you should.

Help each other. Show you care.
Do your best to always share.
Others might love Jesus too
when they see his love in you.

Pray with Me:

Dear Jesus, thank you for being so kind and good.
Teach me to be more like you. Help me to show my family and friends
that I love them. Amen.

Jesus Is Coming Back

The Bible Says:

Jesus has been taken away from you into heaven. But he will come back in the same way you saw him go.

Acts 1:11, NIrV

Jesus rose into the sky,
where he lives in heaven up high.
You can talk to him in prayer.
He can hear you way up there!

Even though he went away,
he's also here with you to stay.
He'll come back for you and me.
What a great day that will be!

Pray with Me:

Dear Jesus, I am glad that you are coming back someday and that you are also with me now. Even though I can't see you, I know I can talk to you. Thank you for teaching me in the Bible how to love you, and how to live while I wait for you. In your name I pray, amen.

What Is Faith?

The Bible Says:

Faith means knowing that something is real even if we do not see it.

Hebrews 11:1, ICB

Faith is knowing God is true.
Faith is knowing God loves you.
Faith is knowing God forgives.
Faith is knowing Jesus lives.

Faith is knowing that God cares
and that he will hear your prayers.
Put your faith in God above.
He will give you all his love.

Pray with Me:

Dear God in heaven, I know that you love me and care about me very much. Help me to keep learning more and more about you so that every day I will have more faith in you. In Jesus' name, amen.

Passing Down the Faith

The Ten Commandments

Before the Bible was written, God gave Moses some rules called the Ten Commandments. Moses wrote them on large pieces of stone so the people could read them over and over again. Parents taught these rules to their children. When the children grew up, they taught the rules to their children. And that's how it went for many, many years. Today we can read the Ten Commandments from the Bible, so parents can still teach them to their children and grandchildren.

Based on Exodus 20

God gave the people some rules to follow, because he loved them and wanted them to live in the right way. This is what he told them:

1. You must not have any other god except for me.

2. You must never bow down or pray to gods that are not real.

3. You must always say God's name in the right way. Do not say God's name in a way that does not please him.

4. Remember to keep a special day for God. The seventh day is a day of rest.

5. Obey your mom and dad.

6. You must never kill anyone.

7. When you grow up and get married, you need to love your husband or wife. You must not love another man's wife or another woman's husband.

8. You must not take anything that does not belong to you.

9. Do not tell lies about other people. Always tell the truth.

10. Don't act as if you should have the things that belong to other people. Be happy with what you have.

These are God's rules. God wants you to love him and obey him.

Psalm 23 (NKJV)

David was a shepherd before he became a king. He loved God very much and wrote many of the psalms. Many people love Psalm 23 because David tells how God cares for us all the time—just like a shepherd cares for his sheep.

A Psalm of David

The LORD is my shepherd;
    I shall not want.
He makes me to lie down in green
    pastures;
    He leads me beside the still
    waters.
He restores my soul;
    He leads me in the paths
    of righteousness
    For His name's sake.
 Yea, though I walk through the
    valley of the shadow of death,

I will fear no evil;
    For You are with me;
    Your rod and Your staff, they
    comfort me.
You prepare a table before me in
    the presence of my enemies;
    You anoint my head with oil;
    My cup runs over.
Surely goodness and mercy shall
    follow me
    All the days of my life;
    And I will dwell in the house of
    the LORD
    Forever.

The Lord's Prayer

Jesus wants us to be humble when we pray to God. He doesn't want us to pray in a way that will make others think we are too important. Jesus taught the people how to pray to God. His prayer is in the Bible, and it is called the Lord's Prayer.

Matthew 6:9-13 (NKJV)

Our Father in heaven,
Hallowed be Your name.
   Your kingdom come.
Your will be done
On earth as it is in heaven.
   Give us this day our daily bread.
   And forgive us our debts,
As we forgive our debtors.
   And do not lead us into temptation,
But deliver us from the evil one.
For Yours is the kingdom and the power and the glory forever. Amen.

A Grandmother's Prayer

A Grandmother's Prayer

The Lord's Prayer

Jesus wants us to be humble when we pray to God. He doesn't want us to pray in a way that will make others think we are too important. Jesus taught the people how to pray to God. His prayer is in the Bible, and it is called the Lord's Prayer.

Matthew 6:9-13 (NKJV)

Our Father in heaven,
Hallowed be Your name.
   Your kingdom come.
Your will be done
On earth as it is in heaven.
   Give us this day our daily bread.
   And forgive us our debts,
As we forgive our debtors.
   And do not lead us into temptation,
But deliver us from the evil one.
For Yours is the kingdom and the power and the glory forever. Amen.

Lord, I come to you today
and lift my prayer to you.
Please be with my grandkids,
in everything they do.

Help their little eyes to see
only what is good.
Give them mouths that speak
    the truth
and say the words they should.

Give them ears that listen well;
please help them to obey.
Give them feet that follow you;
don't let them go astray.

Help their minds to understand
the things that come from you.
Give them wisdom through your
    Word
to know what's right and true.

Surround them with your angels,
and keep them in your care.
Help them, Lord, to turn to you
and talk to you in prayer.

As they grow and as they learn,
please teach them right from
    wrong.
And when they face temptation,
Lord, help them to be strong.

Teach them how to love and care
the way you want them to.
Help them to experience
the joy of serving you.

Lord, please bless these little ones
with blessings from above.
Give them faith and give them
    hope,
and fill their hearts with love.

Amen

Children's children are a crown to the aged,
and parents are the pride of their children.

— Proverbs 17:6, NIV

About the Author

Crystal Bowman is a bestselling author of more than seventy books for children, including *The One Year Book of Devotions for Preschoolers* and *My Read and Rhyme Bible Storybook*. She has written numerous I Can Read! books, as well as stories for *Clubhouse Jr.* magazine and lyrics for children's piano music. She is a mentor and speaker for MOPS (Mothers of Preschoolers) and also speaks at churches, schools, and writers' conferences. Whether her stories are written in playful rhythm and rhyme or short sentences for beginning readers, her desire is to teach children that God loves them and cares about them very much. Crystal and her husband live in Florida and have three married children and one granddaughter.